77 Pieces of Poetry

About
Oklahoma

Karen Kay Knauss

Copyright © 2013

Karen Kay Knauss

77 Pieces of Poetry About Oklahoma

All rights reserved

No portion of this book may be reproduced in any manner whatsoever without written permission from the publisher, except for brief excerpts for review purposes.

Cover Photograph: **Claude Elmore Knauss**
Cover Production: **J. T. Harrison**
Cover Design: **Karen Kay Knauss**
Author Photograph: **Kathy Knauss McCullar**

Peach Tree Press
peachtreepress@pldi.net
ISBN: 978-0-9895926-2-8

Preface

77 Pieces of Poetry About Oklahoma is a poetic narrative about the fascinating and rousing history of Oklahoma, from the creation of its first county in the Unassigned Lands of Indian Territory to the last county in the forty-sixth state. Explorers, Native Americans, trappers, cattlemen, and pioneers—the extraordinary men and women with vision and determination—their stories have made Oklahoma's history exciting, enduring, and even personal when one begins to relate to their experiences along the journey of time.

I have chosen the literary art form of poetry to distinguish the remarkable attributes of each county. The selected poetry forms have dictated the length of each poem while emphasizing specific metrical patterns and rhyming schemes. Each composition presents an opportunity to appreciate poetry as well as history.

The captivating stories about the Twin Territories have left me with a profound and enduring pride in Oklahoma.

Claude Elmore and Lector Lillian Hall Knauss

Oklahoma Territory
Fort Cobb, Caddo County
1901 Homestead Claim 0424

"First Families of the Twin Territories"

Dedication

Claude Elmore and Lector Lillian Knauss

For my Grandparents' participation in and contribution to the settlement of Oklahoma, I will forever be proud and grateful.

With little more than a dream of owning his own land, Claude traveled from Hutchinson, Kansas to enter Oklahoma Territory's Great Land Lottery in 1901. He wrote his name on a registration card that was placed in revolving boxes from which the winning envelopes were drawn. After days of waiting under a blazing August sun, his name was finally called out. Claude met the homestead requirements and received his land patent from President William H. Taft shortly after Oklahoma statehood.

With her parents, Jesse B. and Anna McCamey Hall, Lector came to Oklahoma Territory in 1900 and lived a few years at Paradise Township in Payne County, then Fort Cobb where she lived the remainder of her life. In 1907 she rode the Rock Island Line to Edmond, Oklahoma and attended the first Territorial Normal School, later named Central State Normal School. Lector and Claude were married in 1909.

In spite of their personal hardships, crop failures, the Bank Panic of 1907, the Stock Market Crash of 1929, the Great Depression, Dust Bowl Years, and numerous Wars, the 1901 homestead claim still bears the Knauss name in Caddo County, owned now by grandsons Karl Dwight Knauss and Kris Edward Knauss. Claude and Lector's dreams became an integral part of Oklahoma's history—as well as a legacy to the Knauss family.

Contents

Poem Title	County	Page
The Legends Live	Logan	1
Cleveland's Clarion Call	Cleveland	2
Okla Homma Kaunti	Oklahoma	3
Crossings of Canadian	Canadian	5
The Good Land	Kingfisher	6
The Passion of Payne	Payne	7
Cruzaron el Río de Nutria	Beaver	9
Lincoln's Legacy	Lincoln	10
They Keep the Fire	Pottawatomi	11
Western Red Bed Plains	Blaine	12
In the Gypsum Hills	Dewey	13
Antelope Hills in Comancheria	Ellis	14
From Old Day County	Roger Mills	15
Last of Free Land	Custer	16
For the River That Runs There	Washita	17
Across the Red River	Greer	18
A Chance in Caddo	Caddo	19

The Fertile Oxbow Bend	Kay	21
Along the Salt Fork	Grant	22
Castle on the Salt Plains	Woods	23
Those Willing to Stay	Woodward	24
Icons of Early Days	Garfield	25
On the Osage Plains	Noble	26
Bands of Pawnee	Pawnee	27
Winter Counts of Kaigwu	Kiowa	28
Gatherings on the High Plains	Harper	29
Spirit of Geronimo	Comanche	31
Far From Appalachian Homes	Adair	33
Where Eagles Fly	Alfalfa	34
Stations Along the Boggy	Atoka	35
On the 100th Meridian	Beckham	36
Three Rivers on Shawnee	Bryan	37
The Healing Waters	Carter	38
No Heavenly Manna	Cherokee	39
Chahta	Choctaw	40
En la Tierra de Cimarron	Cimarron	41

Number One Slope Mine	Coal	42
In the Neosho Lowlands	Craig	43
Mvskoke	Creek	44
Lenape, the True People	Delaware	45
Steamboats at Tamaha's Ferry	Haskell	46
Stage Stop Mansion	Garvin	47
"Ancient Council Fires"	Grady	49
For Tumbling Waters	Hughes	51
The Easy Ford at Doan's	Jackson	52
La Batalla de las Dos Aldeas	Jefferson	53
In the Arbuckle Mountains	Johnston	54
San Bois, the Woodless Creek	Latimer	55
Sugar Loaf and Canvanal Peaks	LeFlore	56
In Love's Valley	Love	57
On the Ozark Plateau	Mayes	58
Along the California Road	McClain	59
Cultures of McCurtain	McCurtain	61
Following the Washita	Marshall	63
From Georgia to Three Rivers	McIntosh	64

Prairie Paradise	Murray	65
Lower Creek near Three Forks	Muskogee	66
"No-we-ata"	Nowata	67
Opothle Yahola came to Greenleaf	Okfuskee	68
Oki Mulgi, Boiling Waters.	Okmulgee	69
Wah Zha Zhi	Osage	70
Adawe, The Traders	Ottawa	71
Butterfield's Blackburn Station	Pittsburg	72
Past the Delaware Mount	Pontotoc	73
Place of the "Code Talkers"	Pushmataha	74
Along the Verdegris	Rogers	75
Beloved Holati Emarthla	Seminole	76
"ᏍᏏᏉᏯ Ssiquoya"	Sequoyah	77
Formed From the Twin Territories	Stephens	78
The Land Once Called No Man's	Texas	79
The Osage Trace	Wagoner	80
Tillman's Glory Days	Tillman	81
Nellie Johnstone and the Boom	Washington	83
Cathedral Mountain, Crystal Faces	Major	84

Brass Cones and Glass Beads	Tulsa	85
Legacies of Rare Resolve	Harmon	87
Woodlands of the Cross Timbers	Cotton	88
Acknowledgments		92
Poetry Forms		94
References		100
About the Author		102
Works by Author		104

77 Pieces of Poetry

About
Oklahoma

Karen Kay Knauss

The Legends Live

The legends live of Logan Lands.
In eighteen eighty-nine, men ran
To Unassigned Lands that lay in wait.
Rich gifts were offered up in spate.
The Territory soon began.

Of Red Bed Plains and stones of sand
The Cowboy Flats and grassy spans
Of Cimarron and fauna great,
The legends live.

The Capital once claimed was grand.
A style of elegance was planned
Until Guthrie lost the Seal of State.
For prominence they voiced their plaint,
Then vowed their heritage would stand.
The legends live.

Cleveland's Clarion Call

They came from east and west, from north and south
Afoot, on horse, or clinging to a train.
With little more than pockets full of dreams
They ran to Oklahoma's opened land.

The county they would designate as Three
Was chosen as the first to educate.
To stake the land would never be enough.
Another claim was Cleveland's Clarion Call.

The Bixler Bill was signed by Governor Steele
And pioneers of vision met their charge.
They broke the ground for townships, roads, and farms
Then built a splendid university.

Where once was vast and empty wilderness,
An institute of higher learning stands.
Where once was darkness of an empty mind,
The light of knowledge shines brilliantly.

Okla Homma Kaunti

From faraway places
The wandering Clovis, the Folsom
And the ancient dwellers of earthen mounds
Stopped along their way.
Then they went away.
Los explorators and les explorateurs,

>Stopped along their way,
>Then they went away.

Blankets of red and gold covered the plains
And *Redbuds* bloomed in the woodlands,
Valleys, and narrow ravines.
Whitetail fed upon the tender twigs and pinks,
While *Scissortail* danced in daring descent
With the *"Oklahoma Wind."*

>Massive herds of *Bison* grazed unafraid
>Upon the prairies of *Indian Grass.*

Then came many nations, by force or choice,
With hearts enough to stay.
They crossed that Great American River
Between the Eastern and the Western stars.
They came from east and west, north and south,
Following the ancient *Native Cross*

>That shone above the reddest of lands,
>And *"The Oklahoma Hills."*

The land was called the Great American Desert,
Barren Plains, Indian Zone, and No Man's Land.
Still, stakes were driven into its *Port Silt Loam,*
And County Number Two
Was named by the future *Forty-Sixth.*
Tent towns rose high into the *French blue sky,*

    Labor Omnia Vincit,
    Labor Conquers All Things.

The crimson color of the blood
That flowed from *Five Civilized Tribes*
Befits the color of our *"Oklahoma Rose."*
For fear that tears will never dry,
Unfurl our flag, the *calumet and olive branch.*
"Its symbols of peace unite all people."

    Themis, "Justice and Will of the Gods."
    Look down upon us yet.

Crossings of Canadian

The crossings of Canadian,
And those who passed the way
Became the fancy of the West
And legends of their day.

They tell the story of a man
And Chisholm's Cattle Trail.
Jess knew the rivers' easy fords.
Their crossings he unveiled.

Lone trappers carried pelts and robes,
The traders, wares for sale,
And drovers followed level land
Toward the Kansas rails.

The Texas beeves that thundered north
With flankers at their side
Found flat bed ground and watering
The Springs at Cowboy Camp supplied.

Part Scottish and part Cherokee,
Interpreter and guide,
Jess spoke in fourteen dialects—
For peace as one he strived.

The wagon trails, Rock Island lines
And one called Mother Road,
The crossings of courageous men
In legends yet unfold.

The Good Land

*"For the LORD thy God bringeth thee
Into a good land, A land of brooks of water,
Of fountains and depths ,
Springing forth in valleys and hills;
A land of wheat and barley.....
A land wherein thou shalt eat bread
Without scarceness,
Thou shalt not lack any thing in it;....
And thou shalt eat and be satisfied,
And bless the LORD thy God
For the good land
Which He hath given thee."*
    Deuteronomy 8:7-10

The good land
Was opened up in 1889 and '92.
The people rushed to enter in.
Throughout the Red Bed Plains,
Its breaks and prairie flats,
The waters of the Cimarron would flow.
Hardy seeds of grain were sown,
The barley and the wheat.
Stores from bounteous yields
Provided bread for all to eat.
There was no scarceness in the land,
Nor places near and far,
And many have been satisfied.
They blessed the LORD their God,
For the goodness of the land
Which He had given them.

The Passion of Payne

From Fairmount, the fifth of sons came forth.
They called him Davey, the cousin of Crockett.
He stood six feet, plus six inches more.
To the West he went, the drifter known as

>David Payne:
>His passion led the cause,
>A brand new state his claim.
>For patronage we pause,
>Our *Oklahoma Payne*.

Kansas was impressed; Payne soon found his fame:
The purist pioneer, a politician of repute,
A stalwart soldier and Scout of Cimarron.
Prestige preceded the person they called

>*Captain Payne*:
>His passion led the cause,
>A brand new state his claim.
>For patronage we pause,
>Our *Oklahoma Payne*.

The bold *Prince Boomer*, with powers to persuade,
Led colonists to camps, then cast from coveted lands.
In trials, trusted Treaties would not protect
The faithful followers, or the man called

> *Moses Payne:*
> His passion led the cause,
> A brand new state his claim.
> For patronage we pause,
> Our *Oklahoma Payne.*

The state he sought, where still he lies,
Portrays the past and proudly speaks his name.
For Payne's persistence, pardon was prolonged.
The posthumous plaque was promised then to

> *Father Payne*:
> His passion led the cause,
> A brand new state his claim.
> For patronage we pause,
> Our *Oklahoma Payne.*

Cruzaron el Río de Nutria
They Crossed the Beaver River

Across the ocean, to el Oeste,
Francisco sailed toward New Spain.
Mendoza's fame would so impress,
He sought to rule his own domain,
Galicia was his success.

Love for Beatriz was expressed.
Her heart and padre's wealth he claimed
Then with eight children, they were blessed.
Still further north a new campaign,
For Golden Cities he obsessed.

With cota de malla on his chest,
Francisco wandered through the plains.
Across the "Nutria" he pressed.
For barrenness he would complain.
Quivira was Francisco's quest.

The "Turk" contrived at each behest,
The golden stories he dared feign.
For lies, he would not guide the rest
Through Oklahoma lands again.
Francisco left in deep distress.

With haste, the land was ill assessed
Through greedy blindness to obtain.
In Oklahoma's youthfulness
Lay wealth and treasures that remained—
España's claim would never possess.

Lincoln's Legacy

Lincoln was named to honor Abraham.

Ioway, Potawatomi, Kickapoo, Sac and Fox were

Native tribes that received allotments, yet once

County A belonged to the American Indians.

Of white settlements, Chandler became the seat.

Legends tell of Ozark and Shawnee Trails,

Now recognized on the Nation's Register.

Cross Timbers, Red Bed Plains, and Sandstone Hills,

Open ranges, Deep Fork bottom lands, and

U. S. Highway Route 66 became

Nostalgic marks of Lincoln's legacy.

Thorpe and Harris, Belcher and "Two-Gun Bill" were

Youthful heroes of Lincoln, once County A.

They Keep the Fire

They keep the Fire, their Council Fire.
The Potawatami aspire
To keep Three Brothers' ancient law.
Ojibwe and the Odawa,
Alliances that yet transpire.

From salty waters of the East,
The Potawatomi increased
Near waters of Lake Michigan.
They keep the Fire.

"The Trail of Death" brought suffering,
Then grieving with the Kansas spring.
To Oklahoma some would come,
The "Citizens" of sixty-one.
The "People of Three Fires" still sing,
They keep the Fire.

Western Red Bed Plains

Blaine, once County C, was named for James G. Blaine.

Long before the land opening of 1892,

Arapaho and Cheyenne lived on their Reservation

In western Red Bed Plains and low lying Gypsum Hills.

North Canadian and Cimarron cross the plains that would

Eventually include Caddo and Wichita lands.

Canton, Geary, Greenfiled, Hitchcock, Londale, Watonga,

Okeene— all define the county with gins, mills, and lake;

Unincorporated Southard gained fame for its plaster mills.

Noted authors, statesmen, McBride, Donald Duck's voice,

The Walleye Rodeo, Cheese Fair, and Rattlesnake Hunt:

Yearly events and citizens claimed by Blaine County.

In the Gypsum Hills

County D
Lies in the Gypsum Hills,
It is drained by the Canadian
Through the Cheyenne-Arapaho Reservation,
Once lands of the Choctaw, Chickasaw,
The Creek, and Seminole.
County D
Was opened in April
Of eighteen hundred and ninety-two
With settlers from England, Switzerland, and Ireland.
Farmers, merchants, cowboys, and teachers
Built towns, schools, mills, and gins.
County D
Was soon renamed Dewey
To honor Admiral George Dewey,
An inspiration to all the men and women
From many states and countries afar.
The frontier heroes of
County D
Watched others pass on the
Western Trail and California Road
That led herds north, and the gold seekers to the west.
Mail routes, military roads, and rails
Marked the way to Dewey,
County D.

Antelope Hills in Comancheria

Iron Jacket was Chief in Comancheria.
He died in the Battle of Antelope Hills
Along the north bank of the Canadian
That divides the western plains of Ellis.

The legend of a mysterious power
To blow the enemy's bullets away
Was revealed to be a Spanish coat of mail:
Iron Jacket's magic when Chief of Comanche.

For raids throughout Indian Territory
When the California Road led settlers west
Before it was Old Day County, or Ellis,
He died in the Battle of Antelope Hills.

The grassy prairies were level and treeless
Within the Great Plains that lay to the east of
Oklahoma's 100th Meridian
And along the north bank of the Canadian.

The Cheyenne and Arapaho Reservation
Was opened up in eighteen ninety two,
And with statehood, County E was redefined
With borders that divide the western plains of Ellis.

From Old Day County

County F, once part of Old Day County, lies
Upon Oklahoma's High Plains where
The soft rolling Antelope Hills are
Remarkable and unique to Roger Mills.

Upon Oklahoma's High Plains where
The Canadian and Washita flow,
So did the blood of Black Kettle and the Cheyenne.

The soft rolling Antelope Hills were
Coronado's campsite in 1541 and the
Battlefield of Texans and Comanche in 1858.

Remarkable and unique to Roger Mills
Are the Cheyenne-Arapaho Land Run of 1892,
The Bar X Ranch, and artist Augusta Metcalf,

Last of Free Land

It was the last of "free land" runs,
The Cheyenne-Arapaho Opening
Of eighteen ninety-two.

County G was soon to be named
For one the Indians called "Yellow Hair".
He charged at Washita.

From plains and reservation lands
The Territory soon became a state,
The nation's forty-sixth.

Now Custer claims its heritage
In the Gypsum Hills along the Western Trail
And Old Route 66.

Of native sons who call it home,
Thomas P. Stafford left his legacy
To Custer and the world.

He piloted Gemini VI and
Commanded the first lunar module flight
To the moon, aboard Apollo 10.

The "free land" would not be the last
Of exciting and challenging frontiers,
Like Custer County, and the moon.

For the River That Runs There

For the river that runs there,
The county's name its people would declare.
No longer the tribal land,
Oklahoma's Territory would expand.

Prairies of the Osage Plains,
The muddy red Washita River yet drains.
Old historic roads and trails
Traversed the county before the Frisco rails.

Known as County H at first,
When Cheyenne Arapaho land was dispersed.
The land run brought claims anew
That day, April nineteenth, eighteen ninety-two.

Immigrants from Germany
And Russia settled in Washita County,
Early Mennonite Brethren
Sought to educate the young men and women.

Ten incorporated towns
Now boast of Cordell's stately courthouse of renown,
Their Carnegie Library,
Segar Mission School, and the Great Western Trail.

Across the Red River

Pink Mountains rise from the land,
They belong to Oklahoma's Wichitas.
In bold formations they stand
With colors that give one pause.
They belong to Oklahoma's Wichitas.

The Spanish and French would claim
The land soon to be known as Old County Greer.
Mexico and Texas came
As well to claim this frontier,
The land soon to be known as Old County Greer.

Priests and traders often passed,
Remarkable treks on the Great Spanish Road.
Records thoughtfully amassed,
Their stories have since been told,
Remarkable treks on the Great Spanish Road.

Drovers pushed the Texas bevees
Across the Red River, on the Great Western Trail.
They rested neath live oak trees
And feasted on bobwhite quail,
Across the Red River, on the Great Western Trail.

Bison, elk, and wolves returned
To Greer County, rare as Western Fringed Orchids.
Quartz Mountains, by all affirmed,
Have distinctively eroded
In Greer County, rare as Western Fringed Orchids.

A Chance in Caddo

With Rock Island brochures in his pocket,
                          Claude climbed aboard.
He was southbound for the "Great Lottery"
                          Of "Caddo Strip."
He chanced one life for the hope of another,
"The Oklahoma Opportunity."

Claude stood with his brother and thousands more
                          That August day.
The registration cards were drawn by hand,
                          His name was called.
Two hopeful brothers waited side by side,
The Caddo land they claimed would lay the same.

The flick'ring fires soon glowed in evening camps
                          Like prairie stars,
They twinkled bright with youthful hopes and dreams
                          For tomorrow.
Claude rested on his Oklahoma claim
In mid-September, nineteen hundred one.

The luck of the draw would not be enough;
                                    A one-room house,
A team to plow, and water from a well
                                    Were terms to meet.
With little more than willingness to work,
Claude was granted his Deed in nineteen nine.

Five generations share the history
                                    Of Caddo land:
The Domebo site, Red Rock Canyon, Rock Mary,
                                    And Fort Cobb Lake,
Plains and Prairie Indians, their schools and art,
And old Fort Cobb along the Washita.

With neighbors of those early flick'ring fires,
                                    Claude labored there.
The land would yield rich crops and orchard fruits,
                                    Peanuts, and oil.
The people built museums and penned their books.
They honored the names of those who took a chance.

The Fertile Oxbow Bend

French traders and Wichita knew the sites,
Long before it was the Cherokee Outlet.
Three rivers flowed through the Red Bed Plains,
Lands of Nez Perce, Ponca, Kaw, Apache, and Tonkawa.

Long before it was the Cherokee Outlet
French voyageurs and explorers passed through
The Bryson and Deer Creek Sites.

Three rivers flow through the Red Bed Plains:
The Chikaskia, Salt Fork, and Arkansas.
Washungah led the Kaw to the fertile Oxbow Bend.

Lands of Nez Perce, Ponca, Kaw, Apache and Tonkawa
Now claim the Pioneer Woman, 101 Ranch,
The Marland Mansion, and Chilocco's Boarding School.

Along the Salt Fork

Grant County was first known as County L.

Ranchers leased the grassy plains for grazing

Along the Salt Fork of the Arkansas.

Nathan Boone and George C. Sibley explored

The territory of the Cherokee.

Chisholm and Black Dog trails crossed hunting grounds

Of the early American Indians.

Ulysses S. Grant was honored when they

Named the County in eighteen ninety-four, with

The seat at Medford. Tribes and early settlers left behind

Years of rich history from Grant County.

Castle on the Salt Plains

Woods County, known as County M,
    Borders Kansas on the north.
Gypsum Hills roll across the line
    With the Salt Fork of the Arkansas
And the muddy waters of Cimarron.
    Woods was defined in nineteen hundred six.

George C. Sibley and Captain Nathan Boone
    Explored rivers and the Big Salt Plains
Before the Cherokee Outlet was formed.
    Drovers pushed their Texas beeves
Along the Dodge City and Red Fork Trail,
    The western branch of the Chisholm.

Railroads promoted ranching and farming.
    Alva soon claimed the county seat
And built its Castle on the Hill.
    Oklahoma's second Normal School.
Rich Salt Plains and the Little Sahara
    Distinguish the county named Woods.

Those Willing to Stay

In eighteen ninety-three
    The people called their county N,
        The one that would be known as Woodward.

Upon Red Prairies of High Plains,
    Low lying Gypsum Hills roll
        Where Cimarron and Canadian flow.

Native peoples and prehistoric farmers
    Knew the land of once an inland sea.
        It was their home and hunting grounds.

Beneath the plains and grassy prairies,
    Minerals of salt and bentonite were mined
        And Petroleum and gas were well produced.

Bat Caves and Alabaster Caverns,
    Fort Supply, and western trails
        Became the county's heritage.

The Great Depression, Dust Bowl years,
    And Tornadoes of terror
        Devastated, but would not defeat.

Woodward's story is thoughtfully told
    At the Plains Indians and Pioneers Museum,
        History of the west—and those willing to stay.

Icons of Early Days

In absence of waterways
Cattle trails and railroads led in early days.

Twelve mile stops for routed mail
Were Stage Stations along the old Chisholm Trail:

Skeleton, where Enid stands,
And Buffalo Springs, before Bison was planned.

Hunting Grounds of Cherokee
Were opened to claims in eighteen ninety-three.

Farms and stock ranches would grow
Upon grasslands of Garfield, once County O.

Dugouts and prairie soddies
Served until there were homes, schools, and libraries.

From across the Atlantic,
Czechs and Germans joined with other ethnics.

Cultures and faiths of many
Melded and came to define the new county.

With great pride, museums display
The icons of Garfield County's early days.

On the Osage Plains

Across the prairies and rolling hills
Native tall grasses grow
On the Osage Plains.

From the eastern slopes of the Rockies
The Arkansas flows
As the county's northeastern line.

The Ponca and Otoe-Missouria
Reservations lay in the county
Until nineteen hundred four.

The Cherokee Outlet
Was divided into counties
With the land run of eighteen ninety-three.

Settlers claimed the reservation lands.
Anxious "Sooners" crossed the line early
While cautious "Boomers" waited for the gun.

County P became Noble,
And the "land-office" town of Perry
Became the county seat.

Living fences of the Osage Orange,
Known to natives as bois d'arc,
Defined the territorial farms.

In Oklahoma's "wheat belt,"
Ranchers, farmers, oilmen, and statesmen
Have defined Noble County.

Bands of Pawnee

To the land of Sandstone Hills and Red Bed Plains
The bands of Pawnee came.
The Chaui, Pitahawirata, Skidi,
And Kitkehahki brought their rich history
To the red reservation,
Where they received allotments in ninety-one.

Gordon William Lillie, known as "Pawnee Bill,"
Produced a live show of thrills
And toured the world with stories of the Wild West.
Of state promoters, Bill was one of the best
From Territorial days,
With visions of statehood, museums and highways.

In ninety-four, Pawnee became County Q.
Towns from small villages grew
For the oilmen, farmers, and cattle ranchers.
Prominence was gained from the baseball player,
Moses J. "Chief" Yellow Horse, Evans, Bailey,
And Chester Gould, creator of Dick Tracy.

Winter Counts of Kaigwu

The Winter Counts on sacred bison hides
Were marked with symbols of significance:
The narratives of native Kiowas.
Tohasan's gift passed on to Silver Horn,
The Keepers of the tribal Calendars.

From far Montana's upper Yellowstone
The People drifted south throughout the Plains,
The circle they would paint with shaded blue,
To Oklahoma's Reservation lands,
Near waters of Red River's Northern Fork.

Artistic glyphs were made for every year.
The winter and the summer pictographs
Portrayed the Sun Dance of their gatherings,
The dreadful years of hunger and disease,
And white man's Treaty, sealed with hand in hand.

In nineteen hundred one, the records show
A white man with the section charts in hand,
Divided land, and rounded coins to pay;
Allotments made that early August day,
When Kiowa, by law, was ever bound.

The Territory soon became a state
Where men of many colors live as one.
The Ledger Art and Kiowa of Six,
Colonel Treadwell, Meinert, and Momaday
Bring honors, hand in hand, to Kiowa.

Gatherings on the High Plains

From the Cherokee Outlet, opened up
                                     in ninety-three,
To Woodward County in nineteen seven,
                                     Harper County
Was established in the northwest section
Of Oklahoma, the forty-sixth state.

For their respect of Oscar Green Harper,
                                     The pioneers
Named the land along the Cimarron and
                                     Beaver Rivers.
The Folsom culture and ancient bison
Were revealed at Cooper Bison Kill Site.

The Western Trail was used by cattlemen
                                     In early days,
And troops of the Army's seventh Cavalry
                                     Moved their supplies
On the Fort Dodge to Camp Supply Trail;
Trails known to Cheyenne and Arapaho.

Bison were slaughtered by tens of thousands
                              On the High Plains,
And as far as one could see, lay tons of
                              Bleached bison bones.
Gathered bones were sold for eight dollars a ton,
Or traded for flour, dry goods, and seed.

Pioneers lived in their wagons, then built
                              Houses of sod,
A salt trade, a town of stone, and their own
                              Railway line,
The Buffalo and Northwestern Railroad.
They ranched and farmed above the oil and gas.

Spirit of Geronimo

Two children stood in awe of the small room,
A cell of cold and roughly quarried stones.
The warmth of southern sun was blocked from view
Of one the soldiers called Geronimo.

Why was Apache's famous warrior here,
Their prophet and great man of medicine;
Why did he travel in the Wild West Shows,
And in regalia ride with Roosevelt?

Why was this Fort Sill Base his prison home,
So far from Arizona's mountain lands;
Why was he captive here for twenty years,
On lands near Oklahoma's Wichitas?

Two children stood before the War Chief's grave,
A pyramid of rounded cobblestones.
The words came soft and low from thoughtful babes
With eyes of blue and hair like yellow gold.

Respectfully, they placed their offerings
Among the tokens left by others there:
A jeweled band to glow with evening stars,
And scattered cedar for his safe abode.

The answers for them will not come with ease—
He was a captive in Comanche land.
With childlike innocence, they will perceive
The spirit of the man they call Geronimo.

He lies with his Apache, near Chiefs Knoll
And the Chiefs of Kiowa, Comanche,
And Delaware: Satanta, Kicking Bird,
Quannah Parker, Satank, and Black Beaver.

"I was born on the prairie
Where the wind blew free,
and there was nothing to break
the light of the sun.

There is one God looking down on us all,
we are all the children of one God.
The sun, the darkness and the winds
are listening to what we have to say."

spoken by Geronimo

Far From Appalachian Homes

From districts of Flint and Goingsnake,
Before Oklahoma was a state,
Adair County was formed in the Cherokee
Nation, the choice of its seat had to wait.

In nineteen ten, Stilwell won the seat
Near the Sallisaw and Little creeks.
The "Strawberry Capital of the World"
Brought fame and economic relief.

Boston Mountains are steep with valleys
Of grasslands, where soldiers of Cherokee
Fought on Pea Ridge in the days of Civil War,
East of Indian Territory.

Adair was Wilma Mankiller's home.
The respected leader became well known,
As the first female Chief of the Cherokee,
Far from their Appalachian homes.

Where Eagles Fly

Alfalfa
County belonged to Woods
Till September, eighteen ninety-three
When the vast Cherokee Outlet was opened up
To anxious settlers from lands afar.
Named for "Alfalfa Bill"
And the hay
From the green, grassy plains
Drained by Salt Fork of the Arkansas.
The land once belonged to the Cherokee Nation
Who shared the treasures of Great Salt Plains,
Shown to the first white man,
George Sibley,
In eighteen eleven.
Thousands search for crystal selenite
And watch eagles fly within the Wildlife Refuge.
The pride of generations remains
For the county they named
Alfalfa.

Stations along the Boggy

Captain Atoka led a party of the Choctaw
From their former homes in Mississippi
To the lands that would become Oklahoma.

Atoka was the name of the county
And its designated seat as well
Before statehood of the Indian Territory.

The tribal government was dispelled,
The sovereignty of the Choctaw Nation,
When with the Curtis Act, they were compelled.

The Butterfield made stops at two stations,
Waddell and Geary; they set along the Boggys
Where the North Creek and Muddy River run.

A Civil War skirmish near Harkin's Springs
Is now known as the Middle Boggy Battlefield.
Confederate soldiers were buried at the Springs.

The eastern Ouachita Mountains would yield
Economic growth from forestry, coal, limestone,
Cattle, and crops in the Coastal Plains fields.

Chief Allen Wright became a well known
Leader of the Choctaw Nation, and the name giver
Of Oklahoma; red people, was the choice of his own.

On the 100th Meridian

At statehood in 1907,
Sections of Greer and Roger Mills
To Beckham County were given.
Governor John Beckham had gained fame,
And with their county, the people honored his name.

The Spanish and French made their claims
Of the Red River's Northern Fork,
And lands that lay in the High Plains.
The Gypsum Hills and native grass
Marked clear the Great Spanish Road.

Cattlemen used the Western Trail,
And the military used Camp Supply Road.
Tracks were laid, and people came by rail,
By old Route 66 Highway,
Bus lines, Interstate 40, and then by airways.

For the county seat, Sayre would win,
And build the Museum of Shortgrass Country
While Erick boasts of the 100th Meridian Museum.
Beckham County claimed the land from
The Cheyenne and Arapaho Reservation.

Three Rivers on the Shawnee Trail

The Blue, the Red, and Washita Rivers
Flow through the rich and fertile Coastal Plains
That lay in Choctaw lands of early days,
When they were removed from Mississippi.

To river bottomlands, eastern Choctaw
Brought plantation culture along with slaves.
Sympathies lay with the Confederacy,
For which choice, their punishment was severe.

Fort Washita was a military post
That stood guard over the Texas frontier.
Fort McCulloch was a Civil War post
And strategic site on the Blue River.

Cotton fields lay in the country of trails,
The Texas Road, Butterfield's Mail Route,
And East Shawnee Trail, the first cattle trail
Across the early Indian Nations.

The Choctaw were eager to educate,
They set up churches, academies, and schools.
The first Normal School was built at Durant,
When still the Indian Territory.

In nineteen seven, the county was formed
With Durant as its seat.
Trails, river crossings, treaties, the railroads,
And then statehood, brought growth to Bryan.

The Healing Waters

The Dodge-Leavenworth Expedition
And Randolph B. Marcy explored
The Arbuckles, Cross Timbers, and Plains.

Natural springs and oil seeps
Were known as good medicine to the
Early Plains Indians in the Territory.

The Five Civilized Tribes
Opened health spas at the
Healing Waters of their oil springs.

The county was named at statehood
In honor of Charles David Carter,
Of Chickasaw and Cherokee descent.

Oil fields were soon discovered
And the Healdton Field was opened
In Carter County in nineteen thirteen.

Ardmore was chosen
As the county seat; it grew into
A trade center for cattle, cotton and oil.

Carter's rich heritage includes
The Carnegie Library, the Black Theater
And the Healdton Oil Museum.

No Heavenly Manna

They were called the Western, or Old Settlers,
From Lower Cherokee tribes in Georgia,
They moved to Indian Territory.
Eventually, it became the home
Of the Eastern and Western Cherokee.

Times of tribulation came that winter
When thousands found no heavenly manna
On the Trail of Tears, neither rest, nor peace.
Led by Ross, they grieved for all they had known,
Yet Cherokee maintained their sovereignty.

Keetoowah and Cherokee headquarters
Portray their histories at Tahlequah,
The Nation's Capital and county seat.
Along the Hills of Ozark and Cookson,
The Cherokee built homes, schools, and cities.

Chiefs John Ross, Stand Watie, William Keeler,
Ross Swimmer, and Wilma Mankiller led
The challenging growth the Nation would meet.
Native citizens of the County
Have brought pride and wealth to the Cherokee.

Chahta

Fort Townson was established to manage
Affairs in the Indian Territory, the Civil War,
And the removal of the Choctaw Nation.

Steamboats traveled up the Red River
To the Public Landing with supplies
Promised to the Choctaw by Treaty.

Under their eighteen thirty-eight
Constitution, laws were enforced
By the units of light-horse men.

Schools were built, and the economy grew
With ranching, farming, and lumber.
Hugo became their commercial center.

In nineteen hundred seventy-one,
The Choctaw were allowed elections for their chiefs.
They adopted a new Constitution in eighty-four.

Hugo is known as Circus City,
The home of Governor William Holloway,
Freckles Brown, Lane Frost, and Todd Whatley.

The Choctaw Nation of Mississippi
Was removed in eighteen twenty; their
History and culture have been preserved in Choctaw.

En la Tierra de Cimarron

In the land of Cimarron,
Dinosaurs and ancient peoples have since gone.

The Spanish and Comanche
Claimed the Province, and controlled the land when free.

Josiah Gregg marked the best
Trail for traders and gold seekers heading west.

Outlaws left tales and traces
Of Robbers' Roost, high up in the Black Mesa.

Rich grasses of early days
Pastured sheep, moved by Mexican pastores.

Comancheros traded goods
On the Santa Fe, where small placitas stood.

Some signed the Rock at Cold Springs,
And sought the safety that Camp Nichols would bring.

The Strip, in eighteen ninety,
Became Beaver County, the Panhandle's three.

In nineteen hundred seven,
From Beaver, Cimarron County was taken.

En la Tierra de Cimarron,
Intriguing legends of its people live on.

Number One Slope Mine

Coal County belonged to the Choctaw Nation
Before Coalgate was chosen as the county seat.
Coal mines were opened in eighteen-seventy,
And the county's history was enriched with culture.

Before Coalgate was chosen as the county seat,
The town was known as Liddle, after William Liddle,
The coal mining camp of Number One Slope Mine.

Coal mines were opened in eighteen seventy,
Immigrants came from Europe and Mexico,
And Amish set up dairy farms and industries.

The county's history was enriched with culture,
Then written about by native Muriel H. Wright,
Inductee to Oklahoma's Historians Hall of Fame.

In the Neosho Lowlands

Craig County
was once the hunting grounds
of Plains Indians. The Cherokee
came to the area of Neosho Lowlands
in the east, and long mounds in the west:
Blue, Notch and Hayrick Mounds.
Cabin Creek
became a Civil War
Battleground on Military Road.
Vinita, known as The Junction, became Craig's seat.
Shawnee and Delaware were moved there.
Soon railroads and white men
came as well.
The economy grew
With farming, ranching, mining and oil.
Worcester and Sacred Heart Schools, Halsell College,
Attucks and Pheasant Hill were schools in
the pioneer days of
Granville Craig.

Mvskoke,

The Creek people are known as Mvskoke.
Opothle Yahola was their respected Chief.
The Upper Creek settled along the Canadian
And the County of Creek was established at statehood.

Opothle Yahola was their respected Chief.
He led ten thousand Creek along the Trail of Tears
From Alabama to the Indian Territory.

The Upper Creek settled along the Canadian,
The North Fork and the Deep Fork River valleys
Within the Sandstone Hills of Oklahoma.

The County of Creek was established at statehood.
The seat was named for "Chief" James Sapulpa
Whose trading post was near Polecat and Rock Creeks.

Lenape, the True People

The Delaware, Lenape, or True People
Lived along the Delaware.

When deceived at the Walking Purchase charade
In the Lehigh Valley of Pennsylvania,

Their ancient tribal lands were lost;
For one hundred thirty years, they were displaced.

They settled in Indian Territory
With the Cherokee Nation.

Their new home lay along the Ozark Plateau
Where the Grand, Elk, and Illinois drain the land.

From Kansas, in eighteen hundred sixty-eight,
Charles Journeycake led the Tribe.

Delaware County was named in honor of
The Tribe in nineteen seven,

And Jay was chosen as its seat. The people
Regained their prominence and autonomy.

After many years, they are
Known as the Delaware Tribe of Indians.

Steamboats at Tamaha's Ferry

Haskell County was tribal hunting grounds
Before Europeans came.
The Choctaw Nation would also claim the land
In eighteen-twenty. Many came by steamboats
That landed at Tamaha's
Ferry landing on the Arkansas River.

The county was named to honor James N. Haskell,
Oklahoma's first governor.
The Principal Chief, Greenwood McCurtain,
Served the Choctaw people and lived at Sans Bois.
Stigler won the county seat,
Coal mining stimulated jobs and railroads.

Forestry, agriculture and tourism
Grew the economy.
Arkansas River's Navigation System,
Eufaula's Dam and Robert Kerr's Reservoir
Created new revenue
For the native countians of Haskell.

Stage Stop Mansion

Blue stem grass grows
On the rich bottomlands
Of the Washita River

That flows through
The Redbed Plains
And Sandstone Hills.

The Wichita tribe,
Then the Chickasaw,
Lived in Garvin County

When Pauls Valley was chosen
As the county seat
In nineteen hundred eight.

The new county was named
For rancher and businessman,
Samuel J. Garvin.

Oklahoma was surveyed
From the county's line
At Initial Point.

Agriculture and ranching
Join with oil production
To bolster the economy,

While the Murray Lindsay Mansion
Stands as a testament
To the Territory's success.

Ancient Council Fires

The Chickasaw Nation was removed from
                            Mississippi homes
To the lands of future Grady County
                            In the Redbed Plains.
Where the Canadian and Washita
Flow across the rolling hills and prairies.

Texas drovers pushed their beeves to railheads
                            On the Chisholm Trail,
And settlers and gold seekers followed Marcy's
                            California Road.
An old military route to Fort Sill passed by
The Blue Goose Saloon near Rush Springs.

The Territorial Tribes gathered at
                            Camp Napoleon,
Verden's Cotton Wood Grove, on the banks of
                            The Washita River.
They declared that "the Ancient Council Fires
Shall be kept kindled and blazing" for all.

In memory of his daughter, Nellie,
                        J. B. Sparks offered
Land from her Chickasaw allotment to
                          The College for Girls,
And Oklahoma's Industrial Institute
At Chickasha, nineteen hundred and eight.

Van Dorn brought death to visiting Comanche
                           Who came to make peace
At the Battle of the Wichita Village, camped
                        along Rush Creek.
The 7BC Ranch and "Caddo Bill" Williams'
Half Moon Ranch remain with vivid images of Grady.

For Tumbling Waters

Red Stick Man, the petroglyph on sandstone,
Was painted long before the Creek Nation,
Thlopthlocco, Kialegee, and
Alabama-Quassarte settled the land.

From the Choctaws' Mississippian homes,
They were removed in eighteen thirty-one.
In future Hughes, the Lower and Upper Creek
Settled along the Little and Canadians.

Settlements of Edward's post and Camp Holmes
Were located near the place soon chosen
As Hughes County's new seat at Holdenville,
Named for the railroad man, James F. Holden.

Wetumka, "tumbling waters", became known
As two of the Creek Tribal Towns' Headquarters.
Growth came when Wetumka's oil fields boomed,
And pride came with the Levering Mission.

From a settlement, Holdenville had grown
Into a thriving town by nineteen one
When railroad lines across the land were built
By the Choctaw, Gulf and Oklahoman.

The southeastern Hills of reddened sandstone,
To Creek and Choctaw Nations were given.
The County's history continues still,
With industries and notable countians.

The Easy Ford at Doan's

When Jackson County was Old Greer
Along the trails that crossed the Red
The drovers pushed with wary fear
Of currents strong and quicksand beds.

Along the trails that crossed the Red
A trading post became well known.
For currents strong and quicksand beds,
The easy ford was crossed at Doan's.

The trading post became well known
To hunters of the buffalo.
The easy ford was crossed at Doan's
By cowboys driving cattle slow.

To hunters of the buffalo
The crossing was a place to rest,
As well as cowboys moving slow
And settlers rushing to the west.

The crossing was a place to rest
While Quannah Parker told his tales.
The settlers rushing to the west
Left letters at the post to mail.

Chief Quannah Parker told his tales—
Red River's risks to him were known.
Wise settlers crossed the ford for mail
Along The Western Trail at Doan's.

Red River's dangers were well known,
And drovers pushed with wary fear
Along The Western Trail near Doan's,
When Jackson County was Old Greer.

La Batalla de las Dos Aldeas

El Wichita y sus bandas,
The Wichita, and its bands,
derrotó a las fuerzas de Ortiz Parrilla
Defeated Ortiz Parrilla's forces
en la batalla de los pueblos gemelos
At the Battle of the Twin Villages,
situada a orillas del río rojo.
Located on banks of the Red River.

Le drapeau de la France ont survolé le village,
The flag of France flew over the village,
le centre commercial fortifié
The fortified trading center
qui a servi les français, Comanche
That served the French, Comanche,
et la bande Taovaya de Wichita.
And the Taovaya Band of Wichita.

The Wichita, known as *Kitikiti'sh*,
the Spanish, the *Great Spanish Road*,
And the French traders, or *"coureurs de bois,"*
Left traces of their cultures in Jefferson County.
The Chisholm Trail served Texas cattlemen.
Then railroads brought settlers to the Chickasaw Nation.
The Territory became the state of Oklahoma,
And Jefferson County was formed in nineteen seven.

In the Arbuckle Mountains

The Chickasaw Nation began
In the Territory
When they signed the Old Town Treaty,
In eighteen hundred eighteen.

In early years of settlement,
They lived on Choctaw lands,
Until their new Nation was formed
In eighteen fifty-six.

The Chickasaw's new capitol,
Built at Tishomingo,
Was named for Chief Tishomingo
Who died on the Trail of Tears.

The county was formed at statehood,
Then named to honor Chief Johnston,
Tishomingo became its seat
And a center for trade.

The Arbuckle Mountains yielded
Minerals and quarries,
The fertile Coastal Plains region
Grew crops and rich grasses.

A National Wildlife Refuge,
The Murray State College,
Gene Autry and "Alfalfa" Bill
Bring Honor to Johnston County.

San Bois, the Woodless Creek

The San Bois Mountains of the Ouachita
Were named by French explorateurs who saw
The creek with woodless lands.
While forest pine, hickory, and oaks
Cover the dark shale and sandstone ridged slopes—
The name for both still stands.

Latimer County was formed in nineteen seven,
To Wilburton the seat was given
In lands of the Choctaw Nation.
The Butterfield Overland Mail Route ran
Through Edward, Holloway, Riddle and
The Pusley Stations.

Coal mining promoted growth of railways
And the economy of early days.
Miners have been honored
At the Lutie Coal Miners Museum,
For its homes, the Colony of Veterans
Continues with pride in Latimer County.

Sugarloaf and Cavanal Peaks

In LeFlore County, from Kiamichi
And Ouachita Mountains, one can see
Where Sugarloaf and Cavanal peaks stand.
The French explored Louisiana lands
Before the Dancing Rabbit Creek Treaty.

From delta regions of Mississippi,
To the ancient lands of the Spiro Mounds,
The Choctaw Nation was moved and settled
In LeFlore County.

Military roads, California's Trail,
And the Butterfield Stage led way to rails,
Then highways. Forestry, agriculture
And coal sustain the economy, where
Dogwoods flower on Winding Stair Mountains,
In LeFlore County.

In Love's Valley

Lorsque Marcy a exploré
La Riviére Rouge, il découvre les
Indiens de Wichita.
When Marcy explored along the Red River,
He discovered Wichita.

When Wichita were removed,
The Choctaw settled there in eighteen thirty.
Then the Chickasaw arrived,
And the land became part of their new Nation,
Formed in eighteen fifty-five.

Chickasaw native, Overton Love,
Settled in Love's Valley near Marietta.
Respectfully, the county
Was given his name in nineteen hundred six
With Marietta as its seat.

Lake Murray, Lake Texoma,
And the Hickory Creek recreation sites
Grain crops, cattle, and pecans,
Falconhead Resort, WinStar, and two museums
Portray the history of Love County.

On the Ozark Plateau

Mayes County was established

At statehood in nineteen hundred seven.

Years before, the land belonged to the Osage,

Eventually, it was acquired by the Cherokee.

Samuel H. Mayes was the Chief of their Nation.

Crops of grain, beans and hay flourished on the

Ozark Plateau, while cattle grazed the Prairie Plains.

Under the leadership of the trader and peacemaker,

Nathaniel Pryor, settlers found stability at

Three Forks; his name was given to the county seat.

Yesterday's legends were Stone, Tincup, Ray, and Belew.

Along the California Road

McClain County was named
In nineteen hundred and seven
To honor Charles M. McClain,
Member of Oklahoma's
Constitutional Convention,
In nineteen hundred six.

The South Canadian River flows
Through the Redbed Plains,
Where French traders and trappers
Were followed by explorers
Long, Gregg, Boone, Marcy
And the Dodge-Leavenworth Expedition.

After the Treaty at Camp Holmes,
Chouteau built his trading post
Along the California Road,
The trail that Marcy blazed
For settlers and gold seekers
Crossing the Territory.

The Chickasaw Tribe claimed the land
In eighteen fifty-five,
And Freedmen ran spreads till
The Run of eighteen eighty-nine.
Allotments of the Curtis Act
Made way for the new state.

Purcell, the county seat, was
Set up before the Land Run.
She is called the "Queen City
Of the Chickasaw Nation,"
The "Heart of Oklahoma" and
The "Quarter Horse Capital."

Cultures of McCurtain

The Choctaw Nation was allotted
                       the Coastal Plains
Of the Indian Territory in
                       eighteen twenty.
They were purchased from Louisiana
And lay along the banks of Red River.

Ouachita Mountains are lush with forests
                       Of short-leaf pine,
 Hickory and oak savannah. Rivers
                       That drain the land
Are Red, Little, Mountain Fork, and Glover,
Where whitetail deer, quail, and waterfowl live.

McCurtain County was formed at statehood
                       And named to honor
The McCurtain Choctaw family's three
                       Principal Chiefs.
Wagon trails and ferries were soon replaced
With railroads, bridges and modern highways.

African Americans, Hispanic,
                        Europeans
And Native Tribes brought their varied foodways
                              To McCurtain.
From the wooden mortar and pestle to
Three, split cane baskets, tsalu was prepared.

Wild Onion Dinners served sofky, blue bread,
                            Sweet potatoes,
Fried okra, Hickory nut soup, salt pork
                            And grape dumplings.
Many cultures blended the recipe
For McCurtain County's rich history.

Following the Washita

Indian Territory was the new home
Of the Chickasaw in the eighteen hundreds.

The Texas Road followed the Washita,
And the railroads followed with new settlers.

The rolling prairies of the Coastal Plains
Became Marshall County in nineteen seven.

Land ownership came with the allotment.
Farms and ranches thrived with Statehood.

Madill was voted as Marshall County's seat.
Minerals, farming and ranching brought new growth.

Denison Dam was built on the rowdy Red River,
And Lake Texoma's shorelines promoted tourism.

Oklahoma Governor Raymond Gary
Was the hero of integration and better schools.

Kingston, Madill, and Oakland's economies
Have prospered with oil, industries and tourism.

From Georgia to Three Rivers

Ancient people in petroglyphs
At the Handprint Site, explorers
And traders, followed three rivers:
Deep Fork, the North Canadian,
And Canadian. Lands of the Creek
Since eighteen hundred twenty-eight,
When Chilly McIntosh led them
From their eastern homes in Georgia.

The Engagement at Honey Springs
Allowed a Union victory.
In eighteen hundred sixty-three.
Tribes with divided loyalties
Suffered much during the Civil War.
Creek Chief, Opothle Yahola,
Refused the Confederacy,
Then battled in flight to Kansas.

In eighteen hundred seventy-two,
The MK&T Railroad led to Eufaula,
The county seat named at statehood.
Bottomlands of once fertile fields
In the Creek's Eufaula District
Were covered with Lake Eufaula,
Leaving sandstone hills and timber
Where the Texas Road crossed McIntosh.

Prairie Paradise

Once hunting grounds of the Plains Tribes,
Wichita, Osage and Quapaw,
When the Chickasaw arrived.
They claimed the land from the Choctaw
In eighteen hundred fifty-five.

The Sandstone Hills lie in Murray,
And to the south, the Arbuckles.
Rich grasses grow on the prairies,
Where Washita keeps lands fertile
For farms and ranches in the county.

Davis claims the Falls of Turner,
Marcy's Post and Fort Arbuckle.
Platt National Park, at Sulphur,
Became known for its healing springs,
And named for Chickasaws' honor.

State Governor Roy J. Turner
Built the "Hereford Heaven" cattle ranch
On verdant prairies near Sulphur,
And two were wed at Flying L Ranch,
Dale Evans and Roy Rogers.

At statehood, the county was named
For Governor "Alfalfa Bill"; then
The seat by Sulphur would be claimed.
The Park, Falls, and Lake Arbuckle
Reveal the beauty that Murray still claims.

Lower Creek near Three Forks

Chilly McIntosh led the Lower Creek Nation
From their Alabama homes, forced to abandon,
And settled in Three Forks.
Near the Arkansas, Verdigris, and Neosho
They found the trading post of Auguste Pierre Chouteau,
And guard of Gibson's Fort.

Fort Gibson was their last camp on the Trail of Tears
Yet not the last of the Creek Nation's struggling years
To restore their former life.
Success realized was destroyed by Civil War,
And the Nation was divided, as once before;
They sought to end divisive strife.

The Katy depot was named Muscogee Station,
And the Museum of the Five Civilized Nations
Shares their vivid histories.
With rations, now eight towed barges are allowed,
Arkansas carried Steamboats, the *Swan* and *Grey Cloud*
Once to the Port of Muskogee.

Efforts to establish the State of Sequoyah
Failed, and Muskogee County was formed at statehood
From two territories.
The county has gained prominence for its soldiers,
Superb schools, poets, and statesmen; the Creek
Won back their Nation's sovereignty.

No-we-ata

No-we-ata, from Delaware,
Is to say welcome, or come here.
This name to Metz's first depot,
The county and its seat was bestowed.
The Eastern Delaware live there.

In Verdigris River Valley,
Lie the eastern plains and prairies,
With woodland belts and sandstone hills.
No-we-ata.

Chief Journeycake led Lenape
From Kansas Reservation lands
To Indian Territory.
He served for his people's welfare
On lands bought from the Cherokee,
No-we-ata.

Opothle Yahola Came to Greenleaf

To former lands of the Osage and Quapaw,
Creek were removed from Georgia and Alabama.
The land in Indian Territory
Is drained by Deep Fork and Canadian.
Okfuskee was named for their home of earlier years
In Alabama, before the tragic Trail of Tears.

Tribal towns of Greenleaf and Thlopthlocco
Were settled along the Hills of Sandstone.
Thlopthlocco served as the Civil War headquarters
For Confederate Colonel Douglas Cooper.
Opothle Yahola counseled at Greenleaf for harmony
Between the Creek who served with divided loyalties.

Okfuskee County was established in nineteen seven,
With Okemah as its seat, and towns of Bearden,
Micawber, and Pharoah. Creek slaves were freed
And settled Clearview, Booktree, Rusk, Boley,
And Chilesville. The economy was built on
Farming, ranching, oil, peanuts, and pecans.

Oki Mulgi, Boiling Waters

Twenty-two thousand Creeks were ordered
To endure the dreadful Trail of Tears.

From their homes in Southeastern Woodlands,
The Upper and Lower Creeks were marched west.

The Upper Creeks settled in Indian Territory,
Where the Deep Fork of the Canadian flows.

Unfair and unreasonable treaties, often broken,
Had not deterred the Creeks from serving with loyalty:

The Creek Nation was led by Chief Checote
In the aftermath of the Civil War;

Troop L of the Rough Riders enlisted soldiers
From the Creek and Cherokee Nations;

World War II proclaimed two Oklahoma heroes
Creeks—Richard Bland, and Marty Beaver.

Creek members chose Okmulgee for their capital,
The Lower Creek word, oki mulgi, for boiling waters.

Okmulgee County was established at statehood,
The new state of the Muscogee, the Creek Nation.

Wah Zha Zhi

Wah Zha Zhi,
from the three great rivers,
are "Children of the Middle Waters"
of Missouri, Mississippi, and Arkansas.
They settled on prairies of tallgrass
where the Caney flows through
Osage Plains.
A Nation of three tribes—
the Dwellers from the Upland Forest
led by Chiefs Nopawalla, White Hair, and Claremore—
built villages on the Osage Reserve.
Across fords and woodlands,
Black Dog's Trail
Would become state roadways.
Osage has produced artists, dancers,
Actor Ben Johnson, oil barons, renowned statesmen,
And the Tribal Museum
For Osage.

Adawe, The Traders

South to the Ozark Plateau and Osage Plains,
Chief John Wilson led the Ottawa Tribe
To the lands of Indian Territory
Where the Grand Lake O' the Cherokees lies.

Spear and crafted arrow points, tools, and knives,
Mammouth and mastodon teeth were found near
The Sulphur Springs marsh, on the land that lies
In the Ozark Plateau and Osage Plains.

Cherokee lands were shared with Seneca,
Shawnee, Modoc, Quapaw, Peoria,
Miami, Wyandotte, and the Ottawa.
Chief John Wilson led the Ottawa Tribe.

They belonged to Three Fires Confederacy,
And lived in Canada's Great Lakes region.
The Ottawa were removed to Kansas,
Then to the lands of Indian Territory.

Again, they built their homes, towns, and fine schools.
They prospered in trade and agriculture.
The Ottawa Government was restored
Where the Grand Lake O' the Cherokees lies.

Butterfield's Blackburn Station

The Texas Road and California Route crossed
On lands claimed by the Choctaw Nation,
Whose homes in Mississippi had been taken.

Butterfield's Overland Mail Route crossed
Pittsburg County in eighteen fifty-eight.
Blackburn's Station Site was the old stage stop.

After the Civil War Battle of Perryville,
Union forces burned the town
And the Confederate Army was weakened.

McAlester was named to honor James,
The founder of the coal mining town
That became the Pittsburg County seat.

The coal industry promoted new railroads,
And attracted African Americans,
Immigrants from Europe, and Hispanics from Mexico.

Many workers who lost their lives in mining tragedies,
Are remembered at Chadick Park, and
Mount Calvary's Mass Grave for Mexican Miners.

Pittsburg's economy is supported by
The Oklahoma State Prison, tourism,
And the United States Ammunition Depot.

Thousands come to enjoy Lake Eufaula,
Rich Italian culture, magnificent murals,
Beaches, nature, and Old Town Celebrations.

Past Delaware Mount

The early peoples of Indian Territory
Traveling along the Canadian River,
The Texas, and California Roads
Joined with settlers to form Pontotoc County.

Traveling along the Canadian River
The Quapaw, Wichita, Kiowa, and Comanche
Yielded rolling hills to Choctaw and Chickasaw.

The Texas and California Roads
Led travelers past the Delaware Mount
Through the "cattail prairie" and "Scalp Alley."

Joined with settlers who formed Pontotoc County
The Chickasaw named Ada as the county seat and
Brought honor to their land, rich culture, and history.

Place of the Code Talkers

From homes in Mississippi,
The Choctaw Nation was removed to the West.
Indian Territory
Became the place of renewed growth and success
For the Choctaw Nation living in the West.

Before statehood was declared,
Their capitol was built at Tuskahoma.
The new county formed there
Was named for the Choctaw Chief, Pushmataha.
The Choctaw Museum is housed at Tuskahoma.

Nineteen Choctaw volunteers
Of World War I became known as "Code Talkers."
It would be seven more years
Before the vote was given to the soldiers
Of World War I, the distinguished "Code Talkers".

The Ouachita Mountains lie
Where Little and Kiamichi Rivers flow.
The economy relied
On agriculture, timber, and ranching—
Where "Code Talkers" still whisper in the winds.

Along the Verdigris

The eastern Arkansas Band of Osage
Established Pasuga and Pasona,
Villages in the Three Forks Area
On lands once called the Indian Reserve.
Pasona lay along the Verdigris
Near a mound named to honor Chief Claremore.

His name was known as "Arrow Going Home,"
And his village was called "Place of the Oaks."
In eighteen seventy-one, the village
Was destroyed, and the Osage were removed
To lands along the Verdigris in Kansas.
Cherokee settled in Cooweescoowee

Within the Indian Territory.
The District included Rogers County,
Named in honor of Clement Vann Rogers,
Father of Will, acclaimed speaker and actor.
Indian and white settlers broke the land.
The tall grass prairies and rich bottomlands

Were watered by Caney and Verdigris,
The greenish gray river gathered Caney
And carried goods for five dollars a boat.
From fifteen foot pirogues to eight barge tows,
From landings and posts, to locks and dams,
Verdigris still carries goods to Port of Catoosa.

Beloved Holahte Emathla

They were led by Holahte Emathla
To homes in Indian Territory.
Tribal lands became Seminole County
Where the North Canadian and Canadian flow.

Once the Seminole belonged to the Creek,
The "separatists" moved to Florida
Until the Indian Removal Bill.
They were led by Holahte Emathla.

The Chief signed the Treaty of Fort Gibson
That moved Seminole to the Sandstone Hills.
He died at the end of their harsh journey—
Near the red lands in Indian Territory.

Chief John Jumper signed the treaty that formed
The independent Seminole Nation.
When Oklahoma was declared a state,
Tribal lands became Seminole County.

Wewoka was chosen as the county seat,
Home of Seminole's Capital and Museum.
Oil field industries sustain Seminole,
Where the North Canadian and Canadian flow.

ᏍᏏᏉᏯ *Ssiquoyah*

The Arkansas and Illinois Rivers
Flow throughout the county of Sequoyah.
The bayous, sloughs, bottom lands, and pine trees
Share the land with eastern Plains and Prairies,
Once part of Arkansas' Lovely County.

Sequoyah moved west and joined Old Settlers
From Cherokee homes in lands of Georgia.
His syllabary became "talking leaves,"
The "Tsa la gi Tsu lehisanunhi"
For the Eastern and Western Cherokee.

Osage lands were purchased and delivered
To the Cherokee Tribe from Arkansas.
They moved to Indian Territory
In eighteen twenty-nine. Oklahoma
Honors Sequoyah and the Cherokee.

Formed From the Twin Territories

Jesse Chisholm marked a trail for traders
Through Indian Territory.
It ran from Wichita to Red River
And served the Texas Longhorn drives.

From Chickasaw lands, Stephens was formed
Where Wildhorse Creek crosses Redbed Plains
And drains into the Washita River
Where Beaver Creek drains into the Red.

Education in the Territory
Began with the missionaries,
Then Tribal, common, and subscription schools,
And finally, state public schools.

At statehood in nineteen-seven,
Stephens was formed from Twin Territories—
The Comanche lands in Oklahoma,
And Chickasaw lands in Indian.

Duncan was named as Stephens County seat,
And soon became known as "oil town."
The economy grew with industries
In farming, ranching, gas, and oil.

The Land Once Called No Man's

Upon High Plains within the Great,
The land is flat with rolling hills.
Canadian flows through it still—
As long before it became a state,
Or claimed by men with steadfast will.

The Spanish, French, and Texans failed
To keep the land once called No Man's.
Longhorn cattle grazed on grassy spans
While pushing north on Montana's Trail,
Across the Strip called Public Lands.

The Strip became Beaver County,
And from it, Texas County was taken
In nineteen hundred and seven.
Droughts ravaged the economy,
And Black Sunday darkened the heavens.

Farmers, ranchers, and industry
Produced crops, cattle, oil, and gas.
Treasures beneath the bluestem grass
Brought fame and prosperity
To the Countians of Texas.

The Osage Trace

The Osage Trace became the Texas Road
That soldiers of the Civil War rode upon,
And trail that led the first railroad, "the Katy,"
Across the Creek and Cherokee reserves,
Where Longhorns crossed, and white men came.

Three rivers drain the land—the Arkansas,
The Verdigris, and Grand. Rich prairies lie
With wooded Ozark Hills and pasturelands.
Here, Nathaniel Pryor, Auguste Chouteau,
And Joseph Bogy built their trading posts.

Sequoyah Statehood Bills would be denied.
The County took its place and brand new name
To honor Henry "Bigfoot" Wagoner
And claim with pride—Lt. Col. Childers, Bryan,
Milburn, Hudlin, Linzy, Biffle, and Mr. Bar None.

Tillman's Glory Days

In eighteen-hundred three,
   The future forty-sixth
      Was purchased and surveyed.

The waterways of Red
   Were followed to its source
      On Randolph Marcy's Trail.

The path soon led the way
   For Butterfield's mail route
      And the California Road.

In nineteen-hundred one,
   A lottery was held
      To open southwest lands.

Tillman was then declared
   A county of the state
      In nineteen-hundred seven.

The trails were left behind,
    And "Big Pasture" was sold
        Out of the last frontier.

The county's heritage
    Is colorful and rich
        With Oklahoma lore.

The famous hunt for wolves
    Was shared by two great men,
        Quannah and Roosevelt.

Ramona's Opera House
    Still shines in showplace style
        Of Tillman's Glory Days.

Nellie Johnstone and the Boom

The Caney River and its tributaries
Drain the region of Eastern Lowlands
Where Washington County lies.

Named for U. S. President George Washington
At statehood, the county was defined
As the smallest in the state.

Osage, Western Cherokee, and Delaware
Settled the land with merchants, millwrights,
Farmers, rancher, and teachers.

County orchards, the quarter horse industry,
Prairie hay, and family dairy farms
Produced wealth, as did oil fields.

At Bartlesville, Nellie Johnstone Number One
Was the state's first oil well to be drilled,
And Bartlesville the first oil boomtown.

La Quinta Mansion became Wesleyan University,
Woolaroc became a museum—both represent
The pride of Washington County and its people.

Cathedral Mountain, Crystal Faces

They rise from the Redbed Plains
As in early days of Oklahoma trails
Where the Canadian drains.
Shining Mountains still prevail
As in early days of Oklahoma trails.

Reflecting crystal faces
Are gifts of selenite from an ancient sea.
For men of many races,
Landmarks left behind would lead
With gifts of selenite from an ancient sea.

The mesas and buttes of glass
Are claimed by Oklahoma's Major County.
Ames would yield rich oil and gas
From an unsolved mystery,
Still claimed by Oklahoma's Major County.

West of Cimarron Valley
Cathedral Mountain can be seen from Fairview,
Chosen seat of the county.
Through western skies, clear and blue,
Cathedral Mountain, a landmark the settlers knew.

Brass Cones and Glass Beads

The lands of American Indians
                    Lie in prairies,
Sandstone Hills, and Lowlands of Arkansas'
                    River Valley.
Villages known from seventeen nineteen
Were visited by Jean Baptiste Bénard.

Arrowheads, pottery, deer ulna awls,
                    And bison hoes
Were found together with European
                    Brass tinkling cones,
Glass beads, and gun parts at Lasley Vore's Site,
From the early days in French Territory.

The eastern tribes of Creek and Cherokee
                    Settled the land.
The Lochapoka Creek Band met at the
                    Council Oak Tree
And placed ashes from Alabama's fires,
Where the early Creek village became Tulsa.

Oil was discovered in the Red Fork Field,
                      And then Glenn Pool.
Wildcatters, roughnecks, and tycoons proclaimed
                      "Oil Capital."
Industries of agriculture, cattle,
And aviation brought prosperity.

Tulsa County built universities
                      And colleges,
The Gilcrease and Philbrook Museum of Art,
                      Jazz Hall of Fame,
And the Oklahoma Aquarium,
Where once lay an intriguing wilderness.

Legacies of Rare Resolve

Kiowa, Comanche, Arapaho,
And other Plains Tribes crossed the land when free,
The land once claimed by Spain, France, and Texas.
In 1896, Old Greer became
Part of Oklahoma Territory,
Then in 1907, part of the state.
In '09, the seventy-sixth county
Was taken out of Greer and named Harmon.

The campfires were few, but they were aglow
Upon the unsettled short grass prairie.
Pioneers from afar came with boldness,
Their legacies of rare resolve remain.
Farming and ranching brought prosperity,
Gins, mills, and industry would contribute
To the southwest county's economy.
Of towns that vied for the seat, Hollis won.

Texas was as nearby as a stone's throw,
And on the vast expanse cowboys grazed cattle.
The T-Cross, Hughes. O. M., Rose, and Francis
Were ranches of the west that gained state fame.
Cotton and wheat brought productivity,
And the H & E Railroad carried the freight.
For its sons and daughters—the world would see
The wonders of the county named Harmon.

Woodlands of the Cross Timbers

Cotton County lies upon the grassy plains
Where creeks and streams into Red River drain.
To the east are woodlands of Cross Timbers.
To the south, Red River runs the border,
Once the Native Americans' domain.

Big Pasture was sold with bids by settlers
At the Territory's last land offer.
The state's final county was formed, and named
Cotton County.

The county was named for its cotton production,
And for the county seat, Walters was chosen.
The oil fields brought economic success,
Along with agricultural industry and business.
The Comanche "Code Talkers" hailed from
Cotton County.

Acknowledgments

Ray McCullar
History Department Chair
Oklahoma City Community College

Carl Sennhenn
Oklahoma Poet Laureate
2001-2003

Dr. Ron Gray
Professor of History
Oklahoma City Community College

Kathleen Ann McCullar

Lindel Bailey

I wish to express my appreciation to Ray, Carl, and Ron for their thoughtful reviews of the manuscript *77 Pieces of Poetry About Oklahoma,* as well as their comments of approval. Kathy has been my loyal consultant during this endeavor, encouraging me from its inception; also, to Lindel for his patience and thoughtfulness the past year, especially for all the delightful dinners out.

POETRY FORMS

Poem Title	Form
The Legends Live	Rondeau
Cleveland's Clarion Call	Blank Verse
Okla Homma Kaunti	Free Verse
Crossings of Canadian	Ballad
The Good Land	Free Verse
The Passion of Payne	Bob and Wheel
Cruzaron el Río de Nutria	Quintilla
Lincoln's Legacy	Acrostic
They Keep the Fire	Rondeau
Western Red Bed Plains	Acrostic
In the Gypsum Hills	Triquain Swirl
Antelope Hills in Comancheria	Quintet
From Old Day County	Trimeric
Last of Free Land	Tercet

For the River That Runs There	Sylva Form IV
Across the Red River	Lira
A Chance in Caddo	Sestet Nonce
The Fertile Oxbow Bend	Trimeric
Along the Salt Fork	Acrostic
Castle on the Salt Plains	Sestet
Those Willing to Stay	Triversen
Icons of Early Days	Silva Form IV
On the Osage Plains	Triversen
Bands of Pawnee	Silva Form II
Winter Counts of Kaigwu	Blank Verse
Gatherings on the High Plains	Sestet Nonce
Spirit of Geronimo	Ode
Far From Appalachian Homes	Gwawdodyns
Where Eagles Fly	Triquain Swirl
Stations Along the Boggy	Terza Rima
On the 100th Meridian	Quintilla

Three Rivers on the Shawnee Trail	Quatrain
The Healing Waters	Tercet
No Heavenly Manna	Rimas Dissolutas
Chahta	Triplet
En la Tierra de Cimarron	Silva Form IV
Number One Slope Mine	Trimeric
In the Neosho Lowlands	Triquain Swirl
Mvskoke	Trimeric
Lenape, the True People	Silva, Form II
Steamboats at Tamaha's Ferry	Silva Form II
Stage Stop Mansion	Tercet
"Ancient Council Fires"	Sestet Nonce Stanzas
For Tumbling Waters	Rimas Dissolutas
The Easy Ford at Doan's	Pantoum
La Batalla de las Dos Aldeas	Octave
In the Arbuckle Mountains	Fourteener
San Bois, the Woodless Creek	Rime Couée

Sugar Loaf and Canvanal Peaks	Rondeau
In Love's Valley	Cancione Nonce
On the Ozark Plateau	Acrostic
Along the California Road	Sestet
Cultures of McCurtain	Sestet Nonce Stanzas
Following the Washita	Couplet
From Georgia to McIntosh	Octave
Prairie Paradise	Quintilla
Lower Creek Near Three Rivers	Rime Couée
"No-we-ata"	Rondeau
Opothle Yahola came to Greenleaf	Sestet
Oki Mulgi, Boiling Waters.	Couplet
Wah zha zhi	Triquain Swirl
Adawe, The Traders	Glose Nonce Form
Butterfield's Blackburn Station	Tercet
Past the Delaware Mount	Trimeric
Place of the "Code Talkers"	Lira

Along the Verdegris	Sestet
Beloved Holati Emarthla	Glose Nonce Form
"ᎤᏆᏌᎦ *Ssiquoya*"	Rimas Dissoulas
Formed From the Twin Territories	Ballad
The Land Once Called No Man's	Quintilla
The Osage Trace	Quintet
Tillman's Glory Days	Triplet
Nellie Johnstone and the Boom	Tercet
Cathedral Mountain and Crystal Faces	Lira
Brass Cones and Glass Beads	Sestet Nonce
Legacies of Rare Resolve	Rimas Dissolutas
Woodlands of the Cross Timbers	Rondeau

References

Arrell Morgan Gibson, *Oklahoma, A History of Five Centuries*, Second Edition, University of Oklahoma Press: Norman and London ©1965 by Harlow Publishing Corporation

Foreman, Grant, *The Five Civilized Tribes*, University of Oklahoma Press©1934.

Dorman, Robert L., *It Happened In Oklahoma*, Morris Book Publishing, LLC ©2006.

Wright, Muriel H., Shirk, George H., & Franks, Kenny A., *Mark of Heritage*, University of Oklahoma Press © 1976 by Oklahoma Historical Society.

Morgan, H. Wayne & Morgan, Anne Hodges,*Oklahoma, A History*, W. W. Norton & Co. Inc.©1984, 1977.

Digital library.okstate.edu/encyclopedia/entries/G/GU 003.html

Muriel H. Wright, *Chronicles of Oklahoma*, Vol 8. No. 3, pg 315-334

Elmer E. Brown, "No Man's Land," <u>The Chronicles of Oklahoma 4</u> (March 1926).

Thundering Herds (Norman: University of Oklahoma Press, 1999).

W. Julian Fessler, <u>"Captain Nathan Boone's Journal,"</u> *The Chronicles of Oklahoma* 7 (March 1929).

Oklahoma Counties: History and Information: e-referencedesk.com

Finney, Whitham D. "Jim", *Along the Banks of the Washita, The Story of a Town*, 1976.

Knauss, Kathleen Ann & Knauss, Karen Kay, *Knauss Family History, 1535-2010*, 2010.

~ 100 ~

KAREN KAY KNAUSS

Karen is a native Oklahoman; she grew up on a farm in Caddo County where her family managed the Knauss Peach Orchard. She studied at the University of Science & Arts of Oklahoma and earned a Bachelor of Arts. Karen has enjoyed careers in teaching, fine art, and music. Her unique hand cast fiber sculptures are exhibited in private and public collections across the United States and in several foreign Countries. She established Sundance Studios, performs in the vocal duo, Heart & Soul, and has devoted decades to the research of her family history. Most recently, she has written two poetry chapbooks and three collections of poems, including,

77 Pieces of Poetry About Oklahoma.

Karen has also co-authored two genealogical chronicles and has received numerous awards for her poetry in statewide and regional competitions.

Works by Karen Kay Knauss

OKLAHOMA COAL FIRES
Collection

The Thorny Truth and Their Civil War
Collection

77 Pieces of Poetry About Oklahoma
Collection

Deep Blue Waters
Chapbook

Leaving *Flatland* by Poetry
Chapbook

KNAUSS FAMILY HISTORY

TRULL FAMILY HISTORY

Chronicles, Co-Author
Kathleen Ann Knauss McCullar

77 Pieces of Poetry About Oklahoma
Peach Tree Press
2013

CPSIA information can be obtained at www.ICGtesting.com
Printed in the USA
LVOW12s0826071013

355683LV00006B/13/P